Questions lovingly answered by:

_______________ & _______________

How do I love thee? Let me count the ways.
I love thee to the depth and breadth and height
My soul can reach, when feeling out of sight
For the ends of being and ideal grace.
I love thee to the level of every day's
Most quiet need, by sun and candle-light.
I love thee freely, as men strive for right.
I love thee purely, as they turn from praise.
I love thee with the passion put to use
In my old griefs, and with my childhood's faith.
I love thee with a love I seemed to lose
With my lost saints. I love thee with the breath,
Smiles, tears, of all my life; and, if God choose,
I shall but love thee better after death.

— Elizabeth Barrett Browning —

What is the one thing that no one seems to have in mind when making plans?

☐ HER REPLY ☐ HIS REPLY   ☐ HIS REPLY ☐ HER REPLY

What was the last book that really influenced you?

☐ HER REPLY ☐ HIS REPLY   ☐ HIS REPLY ☐ HER REPLY

Can you describe what you experienced? Why or why not?

☐ HER REPLY ☐ HIS REPLY   ☐ HIS REPLY ☐ HER REPLY

Why do you ever get annoyed with that song?

☐ HER REPLY ☐ HIS REPLY   ☐ HIS REPLY ☐ HER REPLY

What are your three favorite colors?

☐ HER REPLY ☐ HIS REPLY

☐ HIS REPLY ☐ HER REPLY

How would you describe the feeling of being content?

☐ HER REPLY ☐ HIS REPLY

☐ HIS REPLY ☐ HER REPLY

What would make you most content?

☐ HER REPLY ☐ HIS REPLY

☐ HIS REPLY ☐ HER REPLY

How do you get people to like you?

☐ HER REPLY ☐ HIS REPLY

☐ HIS REPLY ☐ HER REPLY

What is your worst-case scenario?

☐ HER REPLY ☐ HIS REPLY

☐ HIS REPLY ☐ HER REPLY

Do you prefer to dance or to walk around? Why?

☐ HER REPLY ☐ HIS REPLY

☐ HIS REPLY ☐ HER REPLY

How would you describe the feeling of being insignificant and having no good sense of self?

☐ HER REPLY ☐ HIS REPLY

☐ HIS REPLY ☐ HER REPLY

What is the most significant factor you've found that allows you to be successful?

☐ HER REPLY ☐ HIS REPLY

☐ HIS REPLY ☐ HER REPLY

Would you rather be a mouse?

☐ HER REPLY ☐ HIS REPLY   ☐ HIS REPLY ☐ HER REPLY

What first turns you on?

☐ HER REPLY ☐ HIS REPLY   ☐ HIS REPLY ☐ HER REPLY

What is the one thing you can do for humanity?

☐ HER REPLY ☐ HIS REPLY

☐ HIS REPLY ☐ HER REPLY

What's one thing you've been told that you shouldn't do?

☐ HER REPLY ☐ HIS REPLY

☐ HIS REPLY ☐ HER REPLY

How do you go about analyzing your goals, your current performance and your current situation?

☐ HER REPLY ☐ HIS REPLY

☐ HIS REPLY ☐ HER REPLY

What would you do if every decision had an infinite number of possible outcomes?

☐ HER REPLY ☐ HIS REPLY

☐ HIS REPLY ☐ HER REPLY

What are you most ashamed about?

☐ HER REPLY ☐ HIS REPLY

☐ HIS REPLY ☐ HER REPLY

Who do you most despise?

☐ HER REPLY ☐ HIS REPLY

☐ HIS REPLY ☐ HER REPLY

What is the best moment of your life?

☐ HER REPLY ☐ HIS REPLY   ☐ HIS REPLY ☐ HER REPLY

What is the best thing you are willing to give up for a good thing?

☐ HER REPLY ☐ HIS REPLY   ☐ HIS REPLY ☐ HER REPLY

How do you deal with people who are not willing to acknowledge who they are?

☐ HER REPLY ☐ HIS REPLY

☐ HIS REPLY ☐ HER REPLY

What would happen if you could fly whenever you wanted? When would you use this ability?

☐ HER REPLY ☐ HIS REPLY

☐ HIS REPLY ☐ HER REPLY

What's your favorite activity to do?

☐ HER REPLY ☐ HIS REPLY

____

____

____

____

____

____

____

____

☐ HIS REPLY ☐ HER REPLY

____

____

____

____

____

____

____

____

What rituals do you have or hold?

☐ HER REPLY ☐ HIS REPLY

____

____

____

____

____

____

____

☐ HIS REPLY ☐ HER REPLY

____

____

____

____

____

____

____

If you had to choose one thing to say to someone you don't like, what would it be?

☐ HER REPLY ☐ HIS REPLY   ☐ HIS REPLY ☐ HER REPLY

What's your biggest problem now?

☐ HER REPLY ☐ HIS REPLY   ☐ HIS REPLY ☐ HER REPLY

How do you feel when you're alone?

☐ HER REPLY ☐ HIS REPLY

☐ HIS REPLY ☐ HER REPLY

Say something about what you want to say but you're afraid to say it.

☐ HER REPLY ☐ HIS REPLY

☐ HIS REPLY ☐ HER REPLY

What is one thing you hope to achieve with your life?

☐ HER REPLY ☐ HIS REPLY

☐ HIS REPLY ☐ HER REPLY

Say something about the world you're in.

☐ HER REPLY ☐ HIS REPLY

☐ HIS REPLY ☐ HER REPLY

What makes you most ashamed?

☐ HER REPLY ☐ HIS REPLY

☐ HIS REPLY ☐ HER REPLY

The boys were playing video games when… [continue the sentence]

☐ HER REPLY ☐ HIS REPLY

☐ HIS REPLY ☐ HER REPLY

How do you deal with your child's personality issues?

☐ HER REPLY ☐ HIS REPLY

☐ HIS REPLY ☐ HER REPLY

If you had to choose just one celebrity to hang out with, who would it be and why?

☐ HER REPLY ☐ HIS REPLY

☐ HIS REPLY ☐ HER REPLY

If you had to choose one word to describe your cousin, what would it be?

☐ HER REPLY ☐ HIS REPLY   ☐ HIS REPLY ☐ HER REPLY

What is this one thing that gives me the ability to be this good?

☐ HER REPLY ☐ HIS REPLY   ☐ HIS REPLY ☐ HER REPLY

List of things that help me have a stress free life

☐ HER REPLY   ☐ HIS REPLY   ☐ HIS REPLY   ☐ HER REPLY

What is the most important personal trait of yours that you do or do not possess?

☐ HER REPLY   ☐ HIS REPLY   ☐ HIS REPLY   ☐ HER REPLY

Say something about your personality.

☐ HER REPLY ☐ HIS REPLY

☐ HIS REPLY ☐ HER REPLY

How do you deal with people who want to try to cheat on you?

☐ HER REPLY ☐ HIS REPLY

☐ HIS REPLY ☐ HER REPLY

What if you are asked to live somewhere else for the rest of your life? Where would you live and why?

☐ HER REPLY ☐ HIS REPLY

☐ HIS REPLY ☐ HER REPLY

Do you ever feel sad? Why?

☐ HER REPLY ☐ HIS REPLY

☐ HIS REPLY ☐ HER REPLY

What is the one thing all children do perfectly?

☐ HER REPLY ☐ HIS REPLY

☐ HIS REPLY ☐ HER REPLY

If you had to put pick a number that has most significance in your life, what will it be and why?

☐ HER REPLY ☐ HIS REPLY

☐ HIS REPLY ☐ HER REPLY

What would you like to see before the job is done?

☐ HER REPLY ☐ HIS REPLY

☐ HIS REPLY ☐ HER REPLY

Will there be a change in your attitude everytime?

☐ HER REPLY ☐ HIS REPLY

☐ HIS REPLY ☐ HER REPLY

Would you rather be a cat or a human when you grow up?

☐ HER REPLY ☐ HIS REPLY

☐ HIS REPLY ☐ HER REPLY

Who are your favorite actors or artists of all time?

☐ HER REPLY ☐ HIS REPLY

☐ HIS REPLY ☐ HER REPLY

What was your favorite moment in high school? Tell what you remember?

☐ HER REPLY   ☐ HIS REPLY   ☐ HIS REPLY   ☐ HER REPLY

What is something awesome you recently learned about?

☐ HER REPLY   ☐ HIS REPLY   ☐ HIS REPLY   ☐ HER REPLY

What is your greatest athletic achievement?

☐ HER REPLY   ☐ HIS REPLY

☐ HIS REPLY   ☐ HER REPLY

Would you rather know now?

☐ HER REPLY   ☐ HIS REPLY

☐ HIS REPLY   ☐ HER REPLY

What's the strangest present you've ever received?

☐ HER REPLY ☐ HIS REPLY

☐ HIS REPLY ☐ HER REPLY

When was the last time you felt loved?

☐ HER REPLY ☐ HIS REPLY

☐ HIS REPLY ☐ HER REPLY

What's your first reaction when you get your hands on something like that?

☐ HER REPLY ☐ HIS REPLY   ☐ HIS REPLY ☐ HER REPLY

If you had to choose one thing to do today, what would it be?

☐ HER REPLY ☐ HIS REPLY   ☐ HIS REPLY ☐ HER REPLY

What's not worth it?

☐ HER REPLY ☐ HIS REPLY

☐ HIS REPLY ☐ HER REPLY

When was the last time you had a good time?

☐ HER REPLY ☐ HIS REPLY

☐ HIS REPLY ☐ HER REPLY

Describe a time when you decided to seize the day.

☐ HER REPLY ☐ HIS REPLY

☐ HIS REPLY ☐ HER REPLY

What is your favorite thing in a movie?

☐ HER REPLY ☐ HIS REPLY

☐ HIS REPLY ☐ HER REPLY

What is the one thing you wish everyone knew?

☐ HER REPLY   ☐ HIS REPLY

☐ HIS REPLY   ☐ HER REPLY

What is one thing about yourself you'd like to change?

☐ HER REPLY   ☐ HIS REPLY

☐ HIS REPLY   ☐ HER REPLY

Do you think that's enough? Why?

☐ HER REPLY ☐ HIS REPLY

☐ HIS REPLY ☐ HER REPLY

What's it like to sit and stare at the wall of your closet for five minutes?

☐ HER REPLY ☐ HIS REPLY

☐ HIS REPLY ☐ HER REPLY

What's the name of the game?

☐ HER REPLY ☐ HIS REPLY   ☐ HIS REPLY ☐ HER REPLY

Do you prefer friends or family? Why?

☐ HER REPLY ☐ HIS REPLY   ☐ HIS REPLY ☐ HER REPLY

What is one thing that you've missed?

☐ HER REPLY ☐ HIS REPLY   ☐ HIS REPLY ☐ HER REPLY

What's the most important thing that you have to remember?

☐ HER REPLY ☐ HIS REPLY   ☐ HIS REPLY ☐ HER REPLY

I am unbreakable because... (continue the sentence)

☐ HER REPLY ☐ HIS REPLY

☐ HIS REPLY ☐ HER REPLY

Do you ever need the strength of others in your life? Why?

☐ HER REPLY ☐ HIS REPLY

☐ HIS REPLY ☐ HER REPLY

Do you have the best time at work? When was it and what are you doing during that time?

☐ HER REPLY ☐ HIS REPLY

☐ HIS REPLY ☐ HER REPLY

How do you deal with a girl who will yell at you?

☐ HER REPLY ☐ HIS REPLY

☐ HIS REPLY ☐ HER REPLY

Tell about a time you were given or gave flowers.

☐ HER REPLY ☐ HIS REPLY

☐ HIS REPLY ☐ HER REPLY

What's your mentality now?

☐ HER REPLY ☐ HIS REPLY

☐ HIS REPLY ☐ HER REPLY

What did you learn from what happened yesterday?

☐ HER REPLY ☐ HIS REPLY

☐ HIS REPLY ☐ HER REPLY

Tell us something that's missing in your hometown.

☐ HER REPLY ☐ HIS REPLY

☐ HIS REPLY ☐ HER REPLY

If you could go back in time to anything from your past,
when would it be and what would you want to know about it?

☐ HER REPLY ☐ HIS REPLY   ☐ HIS REPLY ☐ HER REPLY

How did you make up your mind to change when no one was
listening?

☐ HER REPLY ☐ HIS REPLY   ☐ HIS REPLY ☐ HER REPLY

How would you feel if you were going to be on a show? Why?

☐ HER REPLY ☐ HIS REPLY

☐ HIS REPLY ☐ HER REPLY

If you had to choose one thing that makes you happiest on vacation, what would it be?

☐ HER REPLY ☐ HIS REPLY

☐ HIS REPLY ☐ HER REPLY

If you were the owner of a horse, what type of horse would you choose to be?

☐HER REPLY ☐HIS REPLY   ☐HIS REPLY ☐HER REPLY

What's the first step you can take to making a difference in the world today? Would you try to feed the hungry, improve the environment, promote peace? How would you start?

☐HER REPLY ☐HIS REPLY   ☐HIS REPLY ☐HER REPLY

Why do you need to do that?

☐ HER REPLY ☐ HIS REPLY

☐ HIS REPLY ☐ HER REPLY

What is your biggest regret from your childhood?

☐ HER REPLY ☐ HIS REPLY

☐ HIS REPLY ☐ HER REPLY

How do you deal with the day-to-day pain?

☐ HER REPLY ☐ HIS REPLY

☐ HIS REPLY ☐ HER REPLY

What are you least proud of today?

☐ HER REPLY ☐ HIS REPLY

☐ HIS REPLY ☐ HER REPLY

Say something that doesn't hurt your feelings.

☐ HER REPLY ☐ HIS REPLY

☐ HIS REPLY ☐ HER REPLY

If you could go back in time, would you still do the things you did before or would you change some of them?

☐ HER REPLY ☐ HIS REPLY

☐ HIS REPLY ☐ HER REPLY

Do you ever feel like crying even if you have no idea why? Why? Why not?

☐ HER REPLY ☐ HIS REPLY

☐ HIS REPLY ☐ HER REPLY

If you were an animal, what would you be?

☐ HER REPLY ☐ HIS REPLY

☐ HIS REPLY ☐ HER REPLY

How would you describe the feeling of being right in the middle of a bad situation?

☐ HER REPLY ☐ HIS REPLY ☐ HIS REPLY ☐ HER REPLY

What is the most significant thing you've learned about yourself lately?

☐ HER REPLY ☐ HIS REPLY ☐ HIS REPLY ☐ HER REPLY

How would you describe the feeling of being fulfilled, comforted, refreshed?

☐ HER REPLY ☐ HIS REPLY   ☐ HIS REPLY ☐ HER REPLY

What makes you feel you're going to win?

☐ HER REPLY ☐ HIS REPLY   ☐ HIS REPLY ☐ HER REPLY

Are you ethically obligated to improve yourself? Why?

☐ HER REPLY ☐ HIS REPLY

☐ HIS REPLY ☐ HER REPLY

Who are your favorite heroes?

☐ HER REPLY ☐ HIS REPLY

☐ HIS REPLY ☐ HER REPLY

What are some common mistakes your kids make when they do bad things?

☐ HER REPLY ☐ HIS REPLY

☐ HIS REPLY ☐ HER REPLY

What do your daughters want in the friendship?

☐ HER REPLY ☐ HIS REPLY

☐ HIS REPLY ☐ HER REPLY

Have you met any people who gave you an unforgettable message? What's the message?

☐ HER REPLY ☐ HIS REPLY

☐ HIS REPLY ☐ HER REPLY

How are you using your time?

☐ HER REPLY ☐ HIS REPLY

☐ HIS REPLY ☐ HER REPLY

What's the most interesting and inspiring thing about your favorite person?

☐ HER REPLY ☐ HIS REPLY   ☐ HIS REPLY ☐ HER REPLY

What are you going to do with the one life you have?

☐ HER REPLY ☐ HIS REPLY   ☐ HIS REPLY ☐ HER REPLY

☐ HER REPLY ☐ HIS REPLY   ☐ HIS REPLY ☐ HER REPLY

☐ HER REPLY ☐ HIS REPLY   ☐ HIS REPLY ☐ HER REPLY

What are the three things you look forward to most every day?

☐ HER REPLY ☐ HIS REPLY   ☐ HIS REPLY ☐ HER REPLY

How would you describe the feeling of being tossed around?

☐ HER REPLY ☐ HIS REPLY   ☐ HIS REPLY ☐ HER REPLY

What is most important to you to help you finish what you're doing?

☐ HER REPLY ☐ HIS REPLY

☐ HIS REPLY ☐ HER REPLY

Do you go with the emotion and not worry? Why?

☐ HER REPLY ☐ HIS REPLY

☐ HIS REPLY ☐ HER REPLY

Describe an experience you had that would be considered a near miss or a brush with disaster.

☐ HER REPLY ☐ HIS REPLY

☐ HIS REPLY ☐ HER REPLY

What was a time someone assumed something about you that was completely wrong?

☐ HER REPLY ☐ HIS REPLY

☐ HIS REPLY ☐ HER REPLY

If you could tell me, what's the one thing you've learned about life?

☐ HER REPLY ☐ HIS REPLY

☐ HIS REPLY ☐ HER REPLY

List of things that make me mad

☐ HER REPLY ☐ HIS REPLY

☐ HIS REPLY ☐ HER REPLY

What is the one thing you do regret?

☐ HER REPLY ☐ HIS REPLY   ☐ HIS REPLY ☐ HER REPLY

What do you dislike about your favorite TV show/book/movie/ etc?

☐ HER REPLY ☐ HIS REPLY   ☐ HIS REPLY ☐ HER REPLY

List of things that you want to try

☐ HER REPLY ☐ HIS REPLY

☐ HIS REPLY ☐ HER REPLY

Would you rather, read your emails; change your email settings; or do neither?

☐ HER REPLY ☐ HIS REPLY

☐ HIS REPLY ☐ HER REPLY

List of things that have been done

☐ HER REPLY ☐ HIS REPLY

☐ HIS REPLY ☐ HER REPLY

Would you rather have a cat than the world?

☐ HER REPLY ☐ HIS REPLY

☐ HIS REPLY ☐ HER REPLY

What do your best friends say that you do right about yourself?

☐ HER REPLY ☐ HIS REPLY   ☐ HIS REPLY ☐ HER REPLY

What is the one thing that makes you different from all your friends?

☐ HER REPLY ☐ HIS REPLY   ☐ HIS REPLY ☐ HER REPLY

If you had to choose one thing that makes your life better today, what would it be?

☐ HER REPLY   ☐ HIS REPLY

☐ HIS REPLY   ☐ HER REPLY

Will you try to be a little more cautious?

☐ HER REPLY   ☐ HIS REPLY

☐ HIS REPLY   ☐ HER REPLY

What is the best thing to eat for midnight snack?

☐ HER REPLY ☐ HIS REPLY

☐ HIS REPLY ☐ HER REPLY

If you could be completely defined by one word or concept, what would it be and why?

☐ HER REPLY ☐ HIS REPLY

☐ HIS REPLY ☐ HER REPLY

What would you do if someone cheated on you?

☐ HER REPLY ☐ HIS REPLY

☐ HIS REPLY ☐ HER REPLY

Would you rather be playing with a robot?

☐ HER REPLY ☐ HIS REPLY

☐ HIS REPLY ☐ HER REPLY

What makes you angry?

☐ HER REPLY ☐ HIS REPLY

☐ HIS REPLY ☐ HER REPLY

What books would you wish to read?

☐ HER REPLY ☐ HIS REPLY

☐ HIS REPLY ☐ HER REPLY

How would you describe the feeling of being cold?

☐ HER REPLY ☐ HIS REPLY

☐ HIS REPLY ☐ HER REPLY

If you could go back in time for a day to tell a younger version of yourself what you know now, what would you tell yourself?

☐ HER REPLY ☐ HIS REPLY

☐ HIS REPLY ☐ HER REPLY

How do you deal with all the extra work?

☐ HER REPLY ☐ HIS REPLY   ☐ HIS REPLY ☐ HER REPLY

What will be the hardest task you need to accomplish?

☐ HER REPLY ☐ HIS REPLY   ☐ HIS REPLY ☐ HER REPLY

How would you go about 'saving the world'? What do those words mean to you? How long would it take? Where would you start?

☐ HER REPLY ☐ HIS REPLY   ☐ HIS REPLY ☐ HER REPLY

Do you believe in serendipity? Why or why not?

☐ HER REPLY ☐ HIS REPLY   ☐ HIS REPLY ☐ HER REPLY

Which do you prefer, inside or outside? Why?

☐ HER REPLY   ☐ HIS REPLY

☐ HIS REPLY   ☐ HER REPLY

What was your defining moment?

☐ HER REPLY   ☐ HIS REPLY

☐ HIS REPLY   ☐ HER REPLY

How would you describe the feeling of being viewed as a loser?

☐ HER REPLY ☐ HIS REPLY   ☐ HIS REPLY ☐ HER REPLY

If you could have one conversation with anyone in the world, who would it be with?

☐ HER REPLY ☐ HIS REPLY   ☐ HIS REPLY ☐ HER REPLY

What is most important to your spiritual growth?

☐ HER REPLY ☐ HIS REPLY   ☐ HIS REPLY ☐ HER REPLY

What do you have there?

☐ HER REPLY ☐ HIS REPLY   ☐ HIS REPLY ☐ HER REPLY

When did you last cry?

☐ HER REPLY ☐ HIS REPLY   ☐ HIS REPLY ☐ HER REPLY

Have you ever thought about what life would be like if you were able to see things from the outside in?

☐ HER REPLY ☐ HIS REPLY   ☐ HIS REPLY ☐ HER REPLY

Think about something really mundane and uninteresting to you, now describe in a way that makes it sound breathtakingly beautiful or fascinating.

☐ HER REPLY ☐ HIS REPLY   ☐ HIS REPLY ☐ HER REPLY

_______________________________   _______________________________
_______________________________   _______________________________
_______________________________   _______________________________
_______________________________   _______________________________
_______________________________   _______________________________
_______________________________   _______________________________
_______________________________   _______________________________
_______________________________   _______________________________

When was the last time that you did something that made stop feeling bad?

☐ HER REPLY ☐ HIS REPLY   ☐ HIS REPLY ☐ HER REPLY

_______________________________   _______________________________
_______________________________   _______________________________
_______________________________   _______________________________
_______________________________   _______________________________
_______________________________   _______________________________
_______________________________   _______________________________
_______________________________   _______________________________

How would you describe your life?

☐ HER REPLY ☐ HIS REPLY   ☐ HIS REPLY ☐ HER REPLY

How do you deal with the fact that the way your body functions is so different from everyone else?

☐ HER REPLY ☐ HIS REPLY   ☐ HIS REPLY ☐ HER REPLY

Where did you go wrong?

☐ HER REPLY ☐ HIS REPLY   ☐ HIS REPLY ☐ HER REPLY

List of things that did not work for me

☐ HER REPLY ☐ HIS REPLY   ☐ HIS REPLY ☐ HER REPLY

List of things that are good and at the same time, bad

☐ HER REPLY ☐ HIS REPLY

☐ HIS REPLY ☐ HER REPLY

Describe a time when you, too, had to be cruel to be kind.

☐ HER REPLY ☐ HIS REPLY

☐ HIS REPLY ☐ HER REPLY

What's your favorite supernatural TV show? Least favorite? Why?

☐ HER REPLY ☐ HIS REPLY   ☐ HIS REPLY ☐ HER REPLY

What is one thing you have in common with the villain in your life?

☐ HER REPLY ☐ HIS REPLY   ☐ HIS REPLY ☐ HER REPLY

If you were in a play, what would your character be like?

☐ HER REPLY ☐ HIS REPLY   ☐ HIS REPLY ☐ HER REPLY

How did you spend your free time? Why?

☐ HER REPLY ☐ HIS REPLY   ☐ HIS REPLY ☐ HER REPLY

What's your first reaction when you hear the phrase "a new generation of leaders"?

☐ HER REPLY ☐ HIS REPLY   ☐ HIS REPLY ☐ HER REPLY

How do you deal when people make fun of you?

☐ HER REPLY ☐ HIS REPLY   ☐ HIS REPLY ☐ HER REPLY

What's a simple way to brighten someone's day?

☐ HER REPLY ☐ HIS REPLY   ☐ HIS REPLY ☐ HER REPLY

What might happen if we did?

☐ HER REPLY ☐ HIS REPLY   ☐ HIS REPLY ☐ HER REPLY

What is one thing a parent wants their child to know about sex?

☐ HER REPLY ☐ HIS REPLY

☐ HIS REPLY ☐ HER REPLY

Would you rather be hated or forgotten? Why?

☐ HER REPLY ☐ HIS REPLY

☐ HIS REPLY ☐ HER REPLY

What were you thinking of when you were younger?

☐ HER REPLY ☐ HIS REPLY

☐ HIS REPLY ☐ HER REPLY

List of things that are no longer allowed

☐ HER REPLY ☐ HIS REPLY

☐ HIS REPLY ☐ HER REPLY

What's the biggest lie you've ever told?

☐ HER REPLY ☐ HIS REPLY

____
____
____
____
____
____
____
____

☐ HIS REPLY ☐ HER REPLY

____
____
____
____
____
____
____
____

How would you describe the feeling of being judged and put down by people?

☐ HER REPLY ☐ HIS REPLY

____
____
____
____
____
____
____

☐ HIS REPLY ☐ HER REPLY

____
____
____
____
____
____
____

Tell about a time when you had a conflict with a close friend.

☐ HER REPLY ☐ HIS REPLY   ☐ HIS REPLY ☐ HER REPLY

Which scene in your favorite movie most accurately represent your life?

☐ HER REPLY ☐ HIS REPLY   ☐ HIS REPLY ☐ HER REPLY

What are the three things you fear the most in your future?

☐ HER REPLY ☐ HIS REPLY   ☐ HIS REPLY ☐ HER REPLY

If you could have a time machine, what would it be like to go back? Where would you go?

☐ HER REPLY ☐ HIS REPLY   ☐ HIS REPLY ☐ HER REPLY

If you had to choose one thing from your childhood that has stayed with you through to now, what would it be and why?

☐ HER REPLY ☐ HIS REPLY   ☐ HIS REPLY ☐ HER REPLY

What's your guilty pleasure?

☐ HER REPLY ☐ HIS REPLY   ☐ HIS REPLY ☐ HER REPLY

Do you think you'll ever be able to live without a smart phone? Why or why not?

☐ HER REPLY ☐ HIS REPLY

☐ HIS REPLY ☐ HER REPLY

If you could make a film based on your life, what would the title be?

☐ HER REPLY ☐ HIS REPLY

☐ HIS REPLY ☐ HER REPLY

Would you rather be a philosopher than a rockstar?

☐ HER REPLY ☐ HIS REPLY   ☐ HIS REPLY ☐ HER REPLY

List of things that you should be seeing

☐ HER REPLY ☐ HIS REPLY   ☐ HIS REPLY ☐ HER REPLY

What is your biggest worry?

☐ HER REPLY ☐ HIS REPLY   ☐ HIS REPLY ☐ HER REPLY

If you had to have a conversation with a stranger for a week, what words would you use?

☐ HER REPLY ☐ HIS REPLY   ☐ HIS REPLY ☐ HER REPLY

Why do you come back here?

☐ HER REPLY ☐ HIS REPLY

☐ HIS REPLY ☐ HER REPLY

What's the best thing you've eaten in the last week?

☐ HER REPLY ☐ HIS REPLY

☐ HIS REPLY ☐ HER REPLY

Would you rather do something you're really not that great at?

☐ HER REPLY ☐ HIS REPLY

____

☐ HIS REPLY ☐ HER REPLY

____

What do you prefer to read in bed?

☐ HER REPLY ☐ HIS REPLY

____

☐ HIS REPLY ☐ HER REPLY

____

What did you teach your daughter/son about being respectful?

☐ HER REPLY ☐ HIS REPLY
☐ HIS REPLY ☐ HER REPLY

What would you say to people who think they've seen your face but haven't?

☐ HER REPLY ☐ HIS REPLY
☐ HIS REPLY ☐ HER REPLY

Which came closest to evoking a feeling of dread?

☐ HER REPLY ☐ HIS REPLY

☐ HIS REPLY ☐ HER REPLY

Which living person do you most despise?

☐ HER REPLY ☐ HIS REPLY

☐ HIS REPLY ☐ HER REPLY

What did you choose to be?

☐ HER REPLY   ☐ HIS REPLY   ☐ HIS REPLY   ☐ HER REPLY

What's something about your life that you regret?

☐ HER REPLY   ☐ HIS REPLY   ☐ HIS REPLY   ☐ HER REPLY

Is your work important to you? Why?

☐ HER REPLY ☐ HIS REPLY

☐ HIS REPLY ☐ HER REPLY

What would you do if it came to the point that you didn't have a choice?

☐ HER REPLY ☐ HIS REPLY

☐ HIS REPLY ☐ HER REPLY

What is the one thing about this moment that stands out to you in a very big way?

☐ HER REPLY ☐ HIS REPLY   ☐ HIS REPLY ☐ HER REPLY

How do you measure the quality of your relationship?

☐ HER REPLY ☐ HIS REPLY   ☐ HIS REPLY ☐ HER REPLY

How did your son/girl feel about their father when they had questions?

☐ HER REPLY ☐ HIS REPLY

☐ HIS REPLY ☐ HER REPLY

How's your attitude this year? Why?

☐ HER REPLY ☐ HIS REPLY

☐ HIS REPLY ☐ HER REPLY

If you could only watch one movie for the rest of your life,
what would it be and why?

☐ HER REPLY ☐ HIS REPLY

☐ HIS REPLY ☐ HER REPLY

Do you live for tomorrow or today? Explain.

☐ HER REPLY ☐ HIS REPLY

☐ HIS REPLY ☐ HER REPLY

What was your moment of joy?

☐ HER REPLY ☐ HIS REPLY

☐ HIS REPLY ☐ HER REPLY

How would you describe the feeling of being caught up in something that was exciting?

☐ HER REPLY ☐ HIS REPLY

☐ HIS REPLY ☐ HER REPLY